LETTER TO MARSHY

or

POSTCARDS FROM THE DREGS

This book is dedicated to
Emily, Vicky, Lewis
and anyone else who knows me...

Also by the same author

Well, er...actually nothing. Although I did once leave a note out for the milkman asking for two extra pints and a strawberry yoghurt.

LETTER TO MARSHY

or

POSTCARDS FROM THE DREGS

An appraisal of BBC Radio Kent's
Pat Marsh and his Mid Morning Muddle

Barbara Trigg

Illustrated by Mic Beer

Published for the Twaddle Party by
MERESBOROUGH BOOKS
1992

Published for the Twaddle Party by Meresborough Books, 17 Station Road, Rainham, Kent. ME8 7RS.

Meresborough Books is a specialist publisher of books about Kent with around one hundred books currently in print. These are listed at the back of this book.

In addition Meresborough Books publish the monthly magazine 'Bygone Kent' which they launched in 1979. The cost in 1992/93 is £1.95 per month from your local bookshop or newsagent, or £21.00 (£26.00 overseas) for twelve issues direct from Meresborough Books by post. A free sample copy will be sent on receipt of a 34p SAE.

The author and publishers are grateful to the owners of copyright material for kindly granting permission for its use in the book. Every effort has been made to trace the authors of contributions included, and thanks and apologies are extended to anyone who for any reason may not have been contacted.

ISBN 0948193 727

Printed in Great Britain by Headley Brothers Ltd Ashford Kent and London

Contents

Introduction

Let me introduce myself.

I am a Radio Fan...

I have always found people so much more real and friendly when I could not see them. Jokes are so much more funny when you can use your imagination and other listeners become an extension of your own circle of friends when they telephone and write to your favourite Radio Station.

Once I started writing to Pat Marsh at his Mid-Morning Muddle on Radio Kent I was hooked.

I kept a copy of the myriad poems and silly letters, stored them under the bed, and now I need a stepladder to even reach the mattress. I have lost count of the number of times I have spilt cocoa over teddy just trying to clamber into bed at night.

So, I feel the time has come to dig out these little gems and share them with you again; I say again because some of them have been read out on the air.

But there is quite a bit of new material, together with puzzles and brain teasers to make sure you do not drift off into a comatose state before you reach the end of the book.

And it was not all written by me. Acknowledgements to all those who have contributed over the years. Some of their material is included and names have been named. (Let us hope, for their sake, the neighbours do not get their hands on a copy of this book.)

So thank you, Pat Marsh, for the inspiration.

Now put the cat out, grab a slice of chocolate cake and a cup of coffee, and read on...

Foreword by Pat Marsh

Every radio programme you hear from the BBC is carefully planned, researched, and produced by a team of highly qualified and experienced professionals committed to their art.

Except one.

The Mid Morning Show is put together by a cast of thousands ...in shops, in offices, in kitchens, in pubs, in lorries, in factories ...and they all have just two things in common —

1. Their unique and off-beat sense of humour and natural curiosity for the odd and unusual.
2. They're all raving mad.

No matter how dull the day, how depressing the news, or how tedious the chores, listeners to the Mid Morning Show find a daily dose of fun and laughter is only a tweak of a dial away...

One thing they can never be sure of is what they'll hear...over the first 2,000 programmes the Mid Morning Mob as they are affectionately known, have been picking up their telephones and found themselves helping to find Keith the stuffed camel, tracking down Catweazle, following a biker up Mount Everest, researching the origin of a Monkeys Wedding, clipping a poodle, learning to juggle, celebrating National Prune Week, and struggling through a phone-in quiz with a lady in labour...

Therefore the next (t.b.c.) pages are all your own work.

In other words, don't blame me!

Meet the Gang (an introduction)

For the uninitiated (or those of you with a rotten memory) here is a brief run-down on some of the characters you will come across in your daily dose of the Mid-Morning Muddle, and cropping up from time to time in the pages of this book.

Pat Marsh
: Presenter, Super-star (Winner of the Silver Award in the New York International Radio Festival). Tries his hardest to create a programme from the chaos and mayhem that surrounds him. Sets competitions, reads letters, interviews guests. Would-be Leader of the Twaddle Party (lost his Deposit so many times — they have given him a nice embroidered purse with shoulder strap to keep it safe). Aspiring opera singer (failed audition). Competitor in the Canterbury Half-Marathon (still running). Available for opening of Supermarkets and the switching-on of Christmas lights. aka; Marshy.

Mrs McTavish
: Resident Agony Aunt. A softly-spoken Scot with an understanding and sympathetic nature. Also mans the switchboard, makes coffee for Marshy, warms up his headphones on cold mornings and runs his bath. Duties include scraping the carpet after one of Mo Meadow's visits.

Mo Meadows
: Farmer, raconteur, and a frequent guest on Pat's show. A true historian, he knows all there is to know about Kent. Has the unfortunate habit of parking his muck-spreader in the car park of the Oast — without bothering to empty it first. Good time to go shopping when he visits, as the High Street is empty.

Rosie Beer
: Resident poet. Reads her own and listeners' peoms. Should make Poet Laureate given time.

Captain Kent
: With his parrot, wanders over Kent burying his treasure and leaving clues for sharp-witted listeners. Despite the clues, no one has actually reported digging up any goodies, so several hundred claimants

11

are now searching for a one-legged sailor with a patch over one eye, and his feathered companion.

Lisa Caleno Not to be confused with CANNELLONI which is a tasty Italian dish. Pat's able and long-suffering personal assistant; she is despatched once a week to some far-flung corner of Kent to supply clues for the weekly 'Where Am I' competition. She can be seen standing in castle moats or clinging perilously to some church steeple muttering vaguely 'Where am I...Who am I...whose round is it...?'

Uncle Joe Regular at the Rat and Handbag public house, and the Oast. Disappeared suddenly about the time Aunt Nellie was last heard of. Was inclined to be a little confused at times and speculation is he has either been captured by aliens or has gone on a crusade to America to collect the nylons and chocolate once promised to his sister by an American soldier in 1942. They never materialised.

One-Legged Tramp Some doubt here as to whether he does actually exist. But the signs are indisputable...the odd shoe left at the roadside, the sightings in far-flung counties and foreign parts of wellies, plimsoles, flip-flops and even the occasional tatty sock.

Wendy Provides an insight into the life of an 'everyday housewife' by means of her weekly diary. The secrets of her man-eating neighbour Beryl are revealed, and she imparts valuable advice on how to keep your man happy and under control. Subscribes to the theory that there are only two places that men should be...and one of them is up the garden shed making shelves.

June Care If there is anything cooking in the kitchen, then 'high-speed, finger tip control' June is responsible. Known to her friends as 'Controllability Care', this super-chef from the Gas Board pops up from time to time at the Oast to rustle up culinary treats and distribute recipes.

Monty Parkin Brings a little culture to the Mid-Morning Muddle every Wednesday. This singer/songwriter from Kemsing displays his talents on the guitar with his weekly rendering of humorous ditties. Had some degree of success recently with his David Mellor Song. Much too good for Marsh's programme really — perhaps he has a crush on Mrs McTavish?

Cassandra

Every Monday you will see this mystical figure huddled in the corner of the studio, tea-towel over her head, muttering into her crystal ball. She foretells the coming week's events for each star sign. Spookily accurate — she once foretold a trip over water for Pat...just before he fell over the fire bucket in the corridor.

Aunt Nellie

One time Assistant to Marshy, and the source of one of the greatest mysteries in the history of Radio Assistants. Indeed, the greatest mystery since Stone Henge (and just as old and twice as craggy, Mrs McTavish was once heard to mutter under her breath). Her sudden disappearance threw the whole Oast House into a state of confusion, as she was the most vital and best loved intermediary between the public and their favourite radio programme. A handsome woman in her prime, and always smartly dressed, she was never seen without her designer hat with its neat upturned brim; and her handbag — in which she carried the starting handle, puncture outfit and portable inflatable garage for the Reliant Robin. It is always hoped that she will reappear one day, and a reward has been offered for any information. (See chapter entitled 'What's Happened to Auntie Nellie?')

The Weather Girls

A marvellous bunch of girls, all hand picked by Marshy, who would dance across the studio floor resplendent in fishnet tights and wellington boots, bringing up-to-the-minute reports of the weather in all corners of Kent. So dazzling were they that Pat would wear his dark glasses when a visit was imminent. In fact, several of the male presenters even hid their eyes as the girls would high-kick, bearing their barometers aloft. Dave Austin used to make a dash for the stationery cupboard because his delicate disposition could not take the excitement.

Mic Beer

Long-suffering husband of Rosie Beer our resident poet. An ex-Marine musician, he has been doodling on his sketching pad for twenty years now (surely it must be full up by this time). His excellent cartoons adorn the pages of this book, and countless other Radio Kent tapes, etc. Recently a runner-up in a world-wide competition, organised by Russia, he is still patiently awaiting his prize of 1,000 roubles (about 47p sterling). His 'proper' job is working on the Channel Tunnel. Which is how he first made contact with Radio Kent when, digging furiously, he took a wrong turning and emerged in the middle of the Oast car park.

The boy stood on the burning deck
His energy all spent.
He had to save the ship somehow
... so he tuned to Radio Kent.

The End of a Romance

I have the strangest feeling
That our big romance is dead.
Why else should we play 'Blind Man's Buff'
On top of Beachy Head?

I suspected it was finished;
Our wild, impassioned fling,
When you took me up hang gliding
And tried to cut the string.

When you promised me an overcoat
I thought 'fur is such fun'.
But it wasn't Mink you had in mind.
You meant a concrete one.

We flew off to Majorca.
You were loving, kind and sweet.
Till you opened up my window
At 30,000 feet.

Unwanted and rejected,
I know, now, how it feels.
As I drove through the Safari Park
You were shouting 'Meals on Wheels'!

We holidayed in Egypt,
And a lump comes to my throat
When I remember how you sold me
For two camels and a goat.

And when we went to Florida
To the famous Aqua-Parks,
You took me water skiing
And swimming with the sharks.

But I still love you darling,
To forgive you I will try.
Would you like another slice
Of this delicious MUSHROOM PIE!!!!!!!!

Quiz Time

A dedicated listener? Or is the radio on just to keep the budgie awake and to stop him falling off his perch into the water bowl?

How much do you know about your Radio Kent Presenter who sits in his miniscule studio for hours at a time playing Max Bygraves records until he is numb at both ends?

Do you really care?

Grab a pen and see how you score in this fiendishly devised quiz:

1. Is the Radio Kent Goodie Bag

   a. A delightful selection of stickers, information and photos of your favourite presenters.

   b. A hamper crammed with bottles of the best vintage wine, smoked salmon and paté de foie gras.

   c. Mrs McTavish

2. The combined height of that stunning duo Pat Marsh and Dave Austin is

   a. 15'3⅝"

   b. No one knows for certain because there is not a room at the Oast large enough to accommodate them both together.

   c. 8'7" (they only *sound* tall)

3. Colin Johnson is well known to listeners to Radio Kent — is it for reading

   a. The News

   b. The Times

   c. Playboy

4. Pat Marsh's legs are often a topic of debate — do you think that

   a. They are rather cute

b. That has just reminded you — you must get some celery for tea.

c. A disaster...they are not even a matching pair.

5. The Kent County Show is the big event of the year. As a visitor, do you go
    a. To visit the Radio Kent tent and be entertained by the presenters.
    b. To visit the tents and be entertained by the animals.
    c. To follow the Pedigree bulls round all day with a bucket and spade, because you are a keen gardener.

6. And the Radio Kent Open Day is a keenly awaited event, and the highlight of the Autumn. Do you go
    a. Because you are interested to see how your local Radio Station functions.
    b. Someone told you there was free wine and sausage rolls.
    c. To see Marsh's legs for yourself and dispel any nasty rumours once and for all.

7. Now, as for the Mid-Morning Muddle — do you think Marshy should
    a. Keep the programme just as it is — the perfect balance of music and guests.
    b. Perhaps play the occasional piece of classical music in the hopes of attracting a more intellectual type of audience.
    c. Get himself a decent day job!

8. Radio Kent publishes a number of books on a wide variety of subjects. Do you buy them because
    a. They are amusing, informative and more entertaining than the TV
    b. They have just re-possessed your TV.
    c. Two of them wedged under the dining-room table leg are just the right thickness to stop it wobbling when you carve the weekend joint.

Now let's see how you scored . . .

19

HOW DID YOU SCORE!

1. a3; b1; c2.
2. a3; b2; c1.
3. a3; b1; c2.
4. a1; b2; c3.
5. a2; b3; c1.
6. a3; b2; c1.
7. a3; b1; c2.
8. a3; b2; c1.

24-17 Well done — obviously a dedicated listener, but don't forget that you can have too much of a good thing. Keep up your visits to the psychiatrist and don't throw away the pills quite yet.

16-10 Do I detect itchy fingers here — switching over to 'The Archers' when you think no one is watching? Do try to be a little more loyal. Who knows, one day you might even win a Goodie Bag!

10-0 SHAME ON YOU! If everyone was like you poor old Marshy would have to go back to doing his old paper round again.

A Letter for all Seasons

SPRING

Dear Pat,

About this time of the year the flood of letters starts; from listeners claiming to have heard the first cuckoo, eaten their first Easter Egg, etc. Well I would like to claim the prize which you offer annually of a ten course gourmet meal in the Executive Dining Hall at the Oast; with panoramic view of the breathtaking River Medway and the bustling cosmopolitan area that is known as Chatham High Street.

Yes...I have seen the first Ostrich of Spring.

It has just gone past my house carrying a Tesco plastic bag... No... hang on... my mistake, it's the woman from No. 23 — the one with the skinny legs and the Yak-skin coat.

Well, never mind. I still claim the prize for seeing the first house with a SOLD board outside.

I won't mention where it is for fear of an invasion of sightseers all curious to see this extremely rare sight. And should the media hear of it, the place will be swarming with reporters and photographers.

SUMMER

Dear Pat,

You were urging your listeners the other day to write and tell you all about their summer holidays, so I thought I would drag myself from the sun-lounger to tell you all about this little corner of Paradise, this undiscovered haven of peace, unspoilt by the trappings of commercialism; unblemished by the invasion of foreign camera-snapping, ice-cream-licking tourists in loud Bermuda shorts and wildly flapping plastic flip-flops.

Yes... I am spending the week in my back garden.

There is so much to see and do in this mini Garden of Eden.

The view from my bedroom window is magnificent. Once I get the grass cut I should be able to see out. And if I balance on top of the wardrobe and use the cardboard periscope that I saved from Andrew and Fergie's wedding — then I can actually catch a glimpse of one of the friendly neighbouring islands (Grain, I think they call it) surrounded by gently undulating waves lapping tenderly over its golden shores, with a fleeting kiss they retreat, like some clandestine lover.

Wasn't that poetic? Comes from one of my old Mills and Boon novels.

The garden here has a plethora of wildlife. (Well, wouldn't you be wild if you swooped down to the bird table only to find a mouldy old stale crust.)

There are plenty of activity sports too.

I put a new string in my old tennis racket last week, and when the kids from next door came to ask for their ball back I pretended I hadn't seen it — so now I have a nice new tennis ball as well.

Then, of course, there are the water sports (actually, it's the outside tap). And delicious local fruit can be plucked mouthwateringly fresh from the tree early in the morning. It has to be early because next door get up at 7.00 a.m., and they tend to be overly-possessive about their Victoria plums.

Yes it really is most pleasant here, and if it would only stop raining I think I could really enjoy myself.

AUTUMN

Dear Marshy,

My goodness! that was a windy one wasn't it. Last Thursday I mean.

A friend of mine was up a ladder at the time, renewing guttering to a house at Folkestone. As a direct result of the Force 10 wind he

22

made the first man-powered crossing of the Channel — and as soon as the Hovercraft are running again he will be back to claim his £10,000.

He also hopes to make the Guinness Book of Records as the first man to cross the Channel clutching a 20 ft ladder and a bag of masonry nails.

My mother was standing at the kitchen window that fateful Thursday when her greenhouse suddenly took flight. She watched agog as it disappeared into next door's garden. But look on the bright side. At least we won't have to endure tomatoes with every meal again this year.

WINTER

C   Is for the Christmas cake
That Mother always burns.

H   Is for Dad's hangover.
(The old fool never learns).

R   Is for the rip-off
In all the shops and stores.

I   Is for imposter.
They can't all be Santa Claus.

S   Is for the socks
That all your aunties buy.

T   Is for the turkey
You're still eating in July.

M   Is for the mess when needles
Drop from off the tree.

A   Is for your Access Card,
And approaching bankruptcy.

Christmas is a time of peace,
Goodwill and joy — I think.

S   Is for... OH SNOWBALLS!
I'm going for a drink!!!!!

Phone Now on 811111111111111111...

The best thing about your local Radio Station is it's only a phone call away.

The Mid Morning Muddle phone line glows red hot when Marshy asks for your votes or funny stories.

Anything from your favourite schoolday memories to what you would most miss about England were you forced to flee hurriedly these golden shores. There have been handy hints from helpful participants on 'how to stop hubby snoring' (pop a peg on his nose), 'how to spot Mr Right' (look out for large bulge in wallet pocket), ways to keep warm in winter (three pairs of bedsocks and Patrick Swayze), and choosing a suitable name for your house (Bomzitit).

Muddlers are always eager to share their experiences. June from Gravesend has met Des O'Connor twice. Sheila has hob-nobbed with Richard Burton and Liz Taylor — supping ale in the local hostelry when they were filming at Penshurst Place some years ago. And Valerie has sat next to Charlton Heston and Michael Caine, with his wife and Bridgette Nielsen in Bordeaux.

However, some experiences are not such joyous occasions. Pity the poor prizewinners such as Jolene, who won a Christmas Tree (complete with toffees). It was biting into a toffee that broke a tooth and sent her scurrying to the dentist. Then there was Ernie who won a first prize in the 'Bowling for a Pig' contest. He took the squealing porcine home, fattened it up and the proceeds of the sale paid for a holiday. At least he fared better than the lady with vertigo who won a flying lesson, or the prize winner of a bottle of wine twenty years ago. It was the first and last thing she has ever won in her life.

We have had to suffer people's weird tastes in food. (And if you are reading this book in colour — then I advise you to switch off at this point.)

Peanut butter and jam is passable if you have any American blood in you, but raspberry jam and kippers would take a bit of swallowing. How about a nice sandwich then? Cold omelette, or condensed milk and fried onion.

Excuse me while I just pop outside for some fresh air!

There was a unanimous vote for Gypsy Tart when the subject of favourite school dinners cropped up. The date Napoleon marched on Russia may have slipped your mind. You may have forgotten the main export of Zamboanga. But who could ever forget Gypsy Tart?'

What do you do to while away the hours in that interminable queue? You know, the one where the little old lady at the Post Office grille is taxing her zimmer frame and buying 3,000 second class stamps (so, she is the one who writes all those fan letters to Mohit Dutta). Unless you can emulate an elephant, and sleep standing up, then you need something to keep your mind occupied.

Davina said she would start a sing-song, and another good ploy suggested was to take along a supply of shoe polish and some brushes and earn yourself a bit of dosh as a 'while-U-wait' boot-boy. But the guaranteed way to shift a queue and ensure rapid progress to the front, is to discuss in a loud voice your contagious, and particularly virulent, disease (it never fails).

Of course, some people can be very cruel. 'What makes you laugh?' brought about the response 'Gillingham Football Club'. 'What would you like to accomplish in the coming year' — 'I would like to learn a foreign language, so that I can understand the Mid Morning Muddle.'

Imagine, if you will, five of your favourite presenters (who, in the interests of public health, will not be named here) forming a group of hunky, dancing poseurs. Bodies glistening from the freshly applied grease scraped carefully from one of June Care's discarded baking trays in the Oast kitchen; clad only in strategically placed Radio Kent Car Stickers. Aim? to incite the ladies of Kent to wild abandoned desire, and bring a new dimension to the world of entertainment.

Chippendales step to one side please, while the fabulous five take centre stage.

But what to call themselves?

Suggestions came flooding in.

The Five Flops... The Bare Necessities... The Medway Bares... The Raw Recruits... The Wee Willie Winkies (does she know something we don't?)... The Wibbley Wobblies... The Midriff Crises (hurtful to the extreme). But Sue from Strood hit the nail right on the head when she suggested Nothing to Declare.

Yes, nature can play some cruel tricks at times!

Finally, here is a short mélange.

SAYINGS THAT COULDN'T POSSIBLY BE TRUE

It's raining cats and dogs.
It really gets up my nose.
Two heads are better than one.
Hard work never killed anyone.
Two can live as cheaply as one.

PHRASES THAT CHILL YOUR BLOOD

Your daughter/son saying 'Dad, can you do me a favour?'
The Boss saying 'Come into the office — I want a word'
I don't want to worry you, but...
You will *never* guess what the cat's done.
The garage mechanic saying 'Ah! *your's* is the red Skoda/Escort is it'

PROBLEMS THE ROYAL FAMILY NEVER HAVE TO FACE

Sitting in a second class railway carriage with a curly cheese and pickle sandwich.
A mountain of ironing.
Putting the dustbin out.
Trying to get an urgent Doctor's appointment.
Searching for a parking space Saturday afternoon in Town.
Double glazing tele-sales people.
Rushing up the garden to take in the washing when it rains.
Deciding between the black T-shirt or the red one, because you can't afford both.

Dying for a Quick Riddle?

A man lives on the eleventh floor of a block of flats.

When he goes shopping he takes the lift down to the street, but on his return he only takes the lift up to the fifth floor — then walks up the stairs for the remaining six floors.

Why?

When Pat posed this puzzler on the Mid-Morning Show he didn't really expect to get a sensible answer.

The letter that arrived in the next post was so sensible, in fact, that one is hard pressed to believe it came from a regular listener; or just some poor unfortunate soul whose dial had wandered off course.

Here is the letter.

The correct solution is at the foot of the page.

Dear Mr Marsh,

I was very interested in your news item this morning concerning the poor unfortunate dwarf who has to walk up six flights of stairs in his block of flats each day because he cannot reach the appropriate button in the lift to take him to the eleventh floor where he lives.

My friends at the DHSS (the Department of Help for the Short and Stupid) assure me there are several ways of overcoming this problem.

When your dwarf goes to the shops on the ground floor he should make sure he puts his shopping in a strong cardboard box, which he can then stand on in the lift. This will not be necessary, however, if he buys some high fibre bread, because if the fibre is high enough he can stand on that.

Other shopping items which can be used in these circumstances include: SPRING water, stockings with a LADDER in them, and a JUMPER.

I think you can see from these positive suggestions that the DHSS is not a heartless bunch of bureaucrats as people often suggest, but is in fact a caring organisation with the welfare of all dwarfs in mind.

Murray Evans, Rochester

SOLUTION:

The man is only 4 ft tall, and consequently can only reach the button which will take him to the fifth floor. He is therefore forced to take the stairs for the remaining six floors.

29

Poets' Corner

Inside every listener is a poet struggling to get out. Here is a selection of some that escaped.

Each morning I fly, with a gleam in my eye
To switch on to Radio Kent.
And after a while, with many a smile
I'm not sure if I'm coming or went!

Now I have been caught, and Pat, it's your fault,
Listening to each word that you utter.
It's no illusion to me that my conclusion must be
That you are an absolute nutter!!

Your Mid Morning Muddle, your prattle and twaddle,
Sends me into laughter no end.
And the things that I do, on instructions from you
Are driving me right round the bend.

So Pat, give a thought, for your fans — as you ought,
'Cause we listen with great jubilation.
And this ode I now send, to Marshy — my friend,
And my favourite Number One Station.

J. Mortlock

BONFIRE NIGHT

Thank goodness it's over,
It went on and on.
The shed is still smouldering
And the greenhouse has gone.
The hedge is much shorter
And the plants are all dead.
The cat's gone astray, and
The dog's 'neath the bed.
The fireworks were lovely,
The sparklers so bright;
But that damnable bonfire
Put up such a fight.

It wouldn't stay small.
It went raving mad!
The sparks went a-flying,
It was all very sad.
The guy disappeared
In ten seconds flat.
We thought it would take
Much longer than that.
The apple tree's 'pruned',
The grass all gone brown.
Yes, we had the biggest
Bonfire in town.

So popular was it
That crowds came to see
The amazing spectacle
Set off by me.
But — safety conscious —
We had it all planned.
With garden hose ready,
And buckets of sand.
We did put it out
But it spoilt the day.
So, NO MORE BONFIRES
Is what *I* say!!

P. Wells

31

My thanks, before I celebrate — while I'm still clear and sober;
For mentioning me this morning, on the 21st October.
Am glad you'll play my record, when it finally comes to light,
But you made one small error, which I feel I must put right.

You say I live in **Newcombe Road**, and it really isn't so.
And if I do not point it out, the truth you'll never know.

You see **N** is for nutcases — that's folk like you and me,

and **E** is for earbending — I'm good at that, you see.

W is for wondering — if you can really read,

And **C** for Carol, well, that's me — on that we're both agreed.

O is for occurrence, and it happens every time.

M is for the mail which you receive, from Barmy Banks, in rhyme.

E is for enlightenment, which I'm compelled to give,

As **N** is for NEWCOMEN, the road in which we live!

When I first heard your slip of tongue, it left me quite amused,
But I'm not young, and must admit, am easily confused.
It's causing me some problems, I've found out, to my cost.
Not knowing where I live, I keep on getting lost.
Well, maybe this will help me out of my sad and sorry plight.
It could well be that both of us will get my address right!

Carol Banks
Sheerness

Pronounced NEWCOMMON, Pat

NEW as in unused
COMMON — as muck (for the want of a better description)

THE SKATER

I was so pleased with my hall floor.
I held my brush with pride.
Admired the perfect varnished sheen...
Then Tiddles rushed inside.

Her little paws slid left, then right
And I had never seen
Such a superb exhibition
Since the great Torville and Dean.

Then as she skated past me,
A blur of 'Gold Oak' stain.
I sighed with resignation
And did it all again.

THE OAST HOUSE CHRISTMAS PARTY

I'll now reveal the sordid truth
Of the capers that went on
At the Oast House Christmas party —
(Then I'll sell it to the Sun)

All the DJ's and announcers
Were there from Radio Kent.
To whoop it up and have a jolly
Time was their intent.

They threw out all the copies
Of 'Sing-along-a-Max'
And filled the shelves with Guinness,
Brown Ale, Bitter and Six-packs.

There was a bottle of Champagne
For the funniest disguise.
Poor Marshy didn't wear one
But he still won the first prize.

Don Durbridge — he fell over.
But it wasn't caused by booze.
His Zimmer frame was nobbled —
Someone loosened all the screws.

Paul James came straight from Panto
As he had the evening free.
He was still dressed as a fairy
So they stuck him on the tree.

And June Care baked some mince pies
With holly on the top.
Everyone agreed, 'They're perfect...
We need an Oast door-stop.'

Dave Austin brought no turkey,
Just an octopus — well done.
He said 'the taste is awful,
But there's a leg for everyone.'

Mo Meadows then suggested
His favourite party game.
Drink a bottle each of whisky,
And try to say your name.

Then a certain, frisky, DJ,
With Mavis, Lil and Mary,
Was discovered in the cupboard.
... But he wasn't 'stationary'.

Pat Marsh completely disappeared
'Midst the chaos and mayhem.
They found him three days later.
He'd been filed under 'M'.

The rafters shook and trembled.
The Oast House blazed with light
As they rocked and rolled and twisted
All day and half the night.

Abandoned, wild, immoral.
They behaved outrageously.
And if there's a party next year
... I HOPE THEY INVITE ME!

Out and About in Kent

Put your brain into automatic pilot and find the hidden Kent towns/villages in the following sentences.

1. 'Hand over the money' demanded the bank robber.

2. 'Take a roll Len, ham or cheese?'

3. He threw the dart for Dave, while his friend went to order another round of drinks.

4. She carefully placed the lint on his graze, telling him it would soon heal.

5. She was faintly amused to see him ardently declaring his love, on bended knee.

6. 'Fresh cream made all the difference to the recipe' she told her friend.

7. 'That fence in the back garden needs renewing' Tony said to his wife.

8. He never drove his horse and cart on bridges because his poor old horse suffered from vertigo.

9. 'That man's tone deaf' exclaimed the music critic.

10. Her nephew was such a sweet boy, and so helpful in the garden.

SOLUTION:

1. Dover
2. Lenham
3. Dartford
4. Linton
5. Marden
6. Deal
7. Newington
8. Tonbridge
9. Manston
10. Herne

Glorious Kent

We Kentish Men and Men of Kent (I am not being sexist here, but Women of Kent doesn't quite have that same fluency, does not trip off the tongue quite so easily — and anyway, I've never seen a pub called the Women of Kent) are very proud of our Heritage.

Far and wide this county, tucked away in the bottom right hand bulgy bit on your map, is synonymous with hops, fruit trees and seaside resorts. The type of resort where you can wear a cardboard hat with 'Kiss Me Quick' emblazoned across the front. Where you can wear a knotted handkerchief on your head, roll up your trouser legs (or if you are of the female persuasion, tuck the hem of your dress into your knicker leg elastic).

So here follows a short history lesson...

Mention the County of Kent to anyone over the age of fifty, and chances are their eyes will grow misty as they recall long, hot, sun-filled days spent with the entire family — from grandma to baby — in the hop fields.

More than a source of income in the days of poverty and depression, for most it was their annual holiday. Something to be looked forward to with great excitement.

But how many know the fascinating story of how hops first appeared in Kent?

Let us go back in time to the eleventh century when England was divided into many separate Kingdoms each under the rule of Kings such as Ethelred the Unready, Frederick the Fearless and Gundrun the Gormless. Our little corner of the South East was under the sovereignty of Walter the Unwashed... don't even ask!

Kent was pig farming country at that time, and Walter (a cruel, uncaring King) was strutting about one particularly impoverished village for the sole purpose of extracting more taxes from the already overburdened peasants.

One scruffy individual threw himself at King Walter's feet and kissed the hem of his robe. Now, considering the fashion of the day was for long garments, and bearing in mind that this was pig breeding country where the aforementioned swine freely roamed the fields, this was indeed the act of a desperate and brave man.

How could he pay more taxes, with fifteen children, three pigs and a very ugly wife to support (although with fifteen children it is difficult to believe his wife was *that* ugly). What could he do with just his meagre plot of land?

But his pleading was in vain. Walter the Unwashed scornfully told him to 'hop it'.

Now the unfortunate peasant, being two turnips short of a harvest, misconstrued this rebuff as a helpful piece of advice. He subsequently sold the three pigs (and the ugly wife) and with the proceeds bought more land and a quantity of hop plants — a strange vine recently brought from foreign lands by returning Crusaders.

The rest, of course, is history, and thanks to a thick peasant and a smelly King, Kent is now the Garden of England.

But although we may be well versed in history, our geography leaves a lot to be desired — as one Mr J. Carley was only too eager to point out:

Dear Mr Marsh,

I am writing on behalf of the people of Peasmarsh to you concerning the gramophonic broadcast you produced on 20th February on Radio Kent.

We received information from agents of ours working undercover in the Lydd, Tenterden and Hamstreet areas about a section of your programme known as Captain Kent's Treasure Chest, where at precisely 8.15 and 27 seconds one of your listeners claimed that Peasmarsh was part of Kent. This information was geographically incorrect. Peasmarsh is in the Rother District in East Sussex, two miles outside of Kent.

Naturally we are highly offended at this remark. Our community unanimously prefer to be recognised in conjunction with the Battle of Hastings, The Seven Sisters, and of course Winnie the Pooh our Patron; and not with Channel Tunnels, Historic Dockyards and Dairy Tops Chocolate Mousses.

Peasmarsh, as it was once known, was a Kentish village in the days of Robbling the Welsh Dragon who had a strange craving for bananas.

Then in the 1880s Napoleon 'Bonecrusher' Bonaparte, Emperor of France and the manager of Paris First XI Football Team, challenged Rye and Romney Marsh to an unfriendly in the English Channel.

The Mayor of Eastbourne slipped Peasmarsh back under the Sussex belt during the match and no one has noticed since.

So you see, we are Sussexarians.

Indeed, in Peasmarsh William of Normandy said those famous words in 1067 — 'Why is your chicken on the road?'

So Captain Kent has drawn the short straw. He cannot bury his spondoodles here. The Rother Super Tanker and U-Boat Club (which meet every Wednesday and Sunday) marks the border, and Captain Kent is on the wrong side.

Yours sincerely,

The Right Honourable, Sir Percival Sebastian D'araveline
The Peasmarsh Association of Public and County Relations

But then Pat received a letter from one Des Pondant, who obviously has a bike... he's been *everywhere*.

Dear Mr Marsh,

The enclosed should be read whilst facing the HIGH HALDEN in the WOODCHURCH of SAINT MICHAELS. This is of course a NEWCHURCH.

I wrote the following sitting on a FAIRSEAT on the CLIFFE by a COOLING BROOK whilst eating a HAM SANDWICH and drinking my WICKHAMBREAUX — WYE? — because if you add music it could be an IDE HILL THONG and make the GREAT CHART; then we would be WELLING.

Bet you think this is a load of STODMARSH. Myself I'm off to LEYSDOWN as I feel NACKINGTON.

He then turns pious:

THE LORDSWOOD PRAYER

Our Father HOO HARTLEY in HEAVERHAM,
HADLOW be Thy name.
Thy KENNINGTON come, Thy WILLESBOROUGH done
On WORTH, as it is in HOADEN.
Give us this HERNE BAY our daily RIVERHEAD
And FORDWICH our trespasses,
As we FORDCOMBE those PLATT trespass ASHURST
And LEEDS us not into TENTERDEN
But DOVER us from ACOL.
For HYTHE is the KINGSTON
The HORTON and the KIRBY
For HEVER and HEVER,
      COWDEN.
              STONE me!!!

Great Mysteries of Life

To some people, the whole of life is a mystery. Some wander through every day in a permanent confused state (no names will be mentioned here for fear of Libel suits).

Some mysteries will never be solved — like the ones below:

Where do seedless grapes come from?

How does a thermos flask know whether to keep things hot or cold?

Why is it, when you empty the washing-up bowl, there is always a teaspoon in the bottom?

Why did God make men so helpless? (why did he bother to make them at all?)

Where does an itch go when you scratch it?

When someone treads on your toe — why do *you* always apologise?

Why is it always the queue *you* choose at the bank or supermarket that moves the slowest?

When you get a hole in your sock — where has the wool gone to?

Why doesn't Superglue stick to the inside of the tube?

What were Barn Owls called before there were barns?

When you drop a piece of buttered toast — why does it always fall butter side down?

Why do your car keys only go missing when you want to go out?

Why don't they put hedges straight through the middle of fields instead of around them? It would save an awful lot of clipping...

Half a Mo

Alongside the hops and the apple orchards, Kent has cultivated its own special product.

Kentish to the very core, he is a wealth of knowledge and folklore on the villages and towns of this history-steeped county.

Yes, Mo Meadows, a regular visitor to the Mid Morning Muddle. His stories are always eagerly awaited and always bring response from the listeners. As illustrated by the following:

Dear Mo,

Whilst researching the Genealogy of my family, some most interesting facts came to light which seem to have some bearing on your own family history.

Apparently, in 1666 at Pudding Lane in the City of London, there stood a small baker's shop. Apprenticed to this trade was a certain Dough Meadows (a name too similar to your own to be mere coincidence).

Taking advantage of the fact that the Master Baker was absent on business elsewhere in the City, the indolent apprentice settled down on a stool in the bakehouse, propped his feet up onto the handle of the oven and drifted away into the warm and welcoming arms of Morpheus.

Now at this point it should be mentioned that Dough Meadows had a wooden leg — the direct result of dropping one of his own Fairy cakes on his foot.

So long did he doze there that the heat from the oven kindled the wooden leg (the summer of 1666 being a particularly long, hot, dry one) and it burst into flames. He awoke, dashed round the bakehouse in a mad panic, setting fire to the curtains in the process. The fire spread rapidly and was soon completely out of control.

There was a fruitful outcome to this tragedy. Whilst stomping about the room Dough Meadows inadvertently put his wooden leg straight through the middle of a doughnut lying on the floor — thus creating the first ring doughnut. To honour this auspicious occasion (and not realising that he was the instigator of the fearsome conflagration) King Charles II presented Dough with a handsomely embellished wooden leg and several acres of land in Kent.

But his fame and fortune were made with the discovery that by running ferociously up and down a ploughed field, the wooden leg made a hole that was just perfect for the planting of potatoes; thus speeding up the whole process and firmly establishing the Meadows as a farming dynasty.

Much Clucking

Much Clucking is a pretty village nestling in the soft undulating Downs of the Garden of England.

Its colourful history is celebrated each year with a week-long festival — The Much Clucking Annual Feather Festival.

The whole village participates, and the occasion is planned months in advance. In fact, barely have the feathers settled from one Festival before plans are inaugurated for the following year.

The celebrations begin with a Grand Parade through the village, setting out from the Broody Hen public house, past the post office, round the duck pond and chicken sanctuary, behind the Much Clucking Home for Retired Gentle-chickens (at one time the parade would pass in front of the Home, but the excitement proved fatal for several of the inmates) then winding slowly through the churchyard, the whole tarrydiddle coming to a grinding halt at their original starting point — the Broody Hen.

The 'Grand Cock' then leads the revellers straight to the bar for refreshments.

Several hours later they will emerge, suitably fortified, for the highlight of the week's festivities... The Great Chicken Run. This ritual is based loosely on the Bull Run held in Spain. The young men of the village will congregate in front of the Church Hall and, at the given signal (three loud clucks) several dozen spritely young chickens are released. The villagers dash the length of the road hotly pursued by the hyperactive hens, and head for the safety of the duck pond.

It's not as dangerous as it might appear, however, although there was an unfortunate incident about three years ago when the vicar slipped on something nasty just outside Ye Olde Tea Shoppe and received several vicious pecks to the dog-collar before he managed to scramble to safety.

Events are staged all through the week.

The local amateur dramatic society perform a Classic. This year it is to be Dickens' 'A Tale of Two Chickens'. And the Church Ladies' Unified Choir of Kapellmeister-music (CLUCK, for short) always entertain on the Village Green with a Concert of popular music. Favourites such as Irving Berlin's Dancing Chick to Chick, I'm Putting All My Eggs in One Basket, and that beautiful ballad popularised by Norman Wisdom — Don't Laugh at Me 'Cos I'm a Fowl.

The 'Largest Egg' competition is always well subscribed to, despite the scandal caused on one occasion when the village Post Mistress entered an Emu's egg that she had filched from the Wildlife Park up the road. Miss Drumsticks is chosen from amongst the Village Maidens with a Silver Eggcup for the winner and six-dozen size 5 eggs for the runner-up. The festivities are actually held to commemorate the Great Fowl-Pest Plague of 1664, when the whole village isolated itself from the outside world in order to confine the pestilence to its own small area. With great personal sacrifice they lived for several months on omelettes and dippy-eggs with soldiers, in order to halt the progress of the terrible scourge.

Their bravery is not forgotten by the villagers of Much Clucking...

Proverbs . . . Updated

A Rolling Stone... earns several million a year.

It's an ill wind... that blows up a Scotsman's kilt.

Too many cooks... make all those boring television cookery programmes.

A stitch in time... means you are probably too old to be jogging.

It's no good closing the stable door... if there is a dirty great pile of manure wedged in the opening.

He who laughs last... probably didn't understand the joke.

There's many a slip twixt... British Home Stores and Marks lingerie departments.

Many Hans... means a coachload of touring Austrians has just arrived.

Still waters... can only mean the top has been left off the Perrier water again.

Half a loaf... is just about all I can afford these days.

Oh, The Agony!

Heartbroken? At your wit's end? Need a shoulder to cry on? Kid's stuffed the cat down the toilet for the fifth time this week? Husband run off with the barmaid... husband *won't* run off with the barmaid?

Whatever your problem you can be sure of a sympathetic ear when you write to Mrs McTavish.

The stalwart Scottish lassie with the shoulders that a caber tosser would be proud of... and a heart the size of a Haggis.

As she says herself; a trouble shared is a trouble doubled. How very profound.

Here are some of the many letters she receives, and some of her worldly wise advice.

Dear Flora,
   HELP!

For the last three weeks now I have been driving round and round the M25 looking for an exit.

What should have been an uplifting and informative evening — a lecture and demonstration on 'Turnip Carving or 101 Things to do with a Root Vegetable', has turned into a circuitous nightmare.

I know Mother must have missed me by now, as every third Friday in the month I trim her moustache and give her false teeth a good going over with a brillo pad.

Luckily, Mother had packed my Mister Men Lunch Box with goodies and a flask; but I am now down to my last Marmite sandwich and starting to get worried.

I listen to Radio Kent all day so do you think you could possibly give me a few helpful directions on your next Agony spot.

LOST LEN

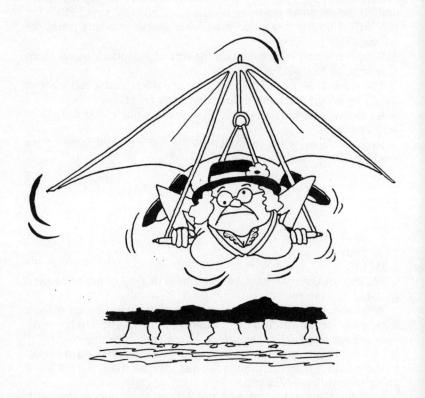

My Dear Flora,

I have trouble with a very loud and complaining Aunt.

Nothing is ever right. She is never happy unless she is unhappy.

Last week I took her to a nice little café for a sandwich and a pot of tea. When she requested a sandwich with meat filling the waitress apologised and explained that tongue was all they had left.

Auntie kicked up a terrible fuss, said how terribly disgusting, and she couldn't possibly eat anything that came from an animal's mouth... she would just have an egg.

When I took her hang-gliding — thinking that a hobby would take her mind off her continuous moaning — she refused to jump off Beachy Head unless she had one of those parachute thingys like mine.

I tell you I cannot take much more of her whingeing.

WEARY OF WESTERHAM

Dear Mrs McTavish,

Could you please advise me how to fight the battle of the bulge and the general disintegration that creeps upon us.

As I approach middle age I still have all my bits, but they appear to have shifted to new positions.

There are bags under my eyes the Post Office would be pleased to use for their Christmas mail, and I have got more spare tyres than a Kwik-Fit Fitter.

I did buy a nice new corset, but in my haste I must have bought a size too small. Every time I cough it rides up. I was in Tesco's last week, had a nasty coughing fit and by the time I reached the checkout I had gone completely deaf and couldn't see a thing.

Hubby used to call me his little peach.

Now he calls me his little peach crumble.

WOBBLY WENDY

Dear Mrs McTavish,

My cantankerous and wilful aged mother is driving us to distraction.

For example; on her 93rd birthday we bought her a lovely new set of dentures. What did she do?... used them to wedge open the back door because she said it makes a nice breeze through her lobby.

Then last Tuesday I called round unexpectedly and found her using the top set to make the crinkly pattern round the edge of a meat pie.

One dreads to think what she used to make the hole in the middle.

WE always have her best interests at heart, but however hard we try it is never appreciated.

FRUSTRATED OF FRINDSBURY

Dear Mrs McTavish,

I desperately need professional help with a problem which is threatening to take over my life.

You see, I have this uncontrollable passion for men in uniform.

I find I am deliberately parking on double yellow lines in the hope that a nice Warden will appear and take down my particulars.

Last week I blatantly threw myself down an open man-hole knowing that someone would summon an ambulance, and that would mean close contact with at least three hunky, rough, blue serge uniforms.

Even the cat is not safe from my devious plotting. On Friday I chased him up a tree with a sharp stick — just so that I could call out the Fire Brigade to get him down again.

The postman refuses to deliver to my house ever since the time I grabbed his hand through the letter box and it took three grown men to prise me off. I tried to blame it on the dog, but I don't think I managed to convince him. Now he leaves my letters next door.

Is there no cure for this addiction?

MARAUDING MAVIS OF MAIDSTONE

Some of the letters that Flora receives are much too personal and revealing to be read out over the airwaves.

Or, indeed, put into print.

It used to be said that you could do anything as long as it did not frighten the horses. But some of Radio Kent's listeners are little old ladies of a delicate nature; and for their sakes I have decided that only the answers will appear:

To 'confused'... Well, it would wouldn't it! You should have waited for the paint to dry.

Tarzan... try a stronger vine, or, alternatively, Halfords do a nice line in towing ropes.

Adam of Little Showin... Surely you can find a bigger leaf — silly boy — write to Bob Collard this very instant!

'Mixed-up' of Marden... I have never heard of that before. Are you sure you haven't got two pages of the Manual stuck together?

'Handyman' of Harrietsham... Well, dearie! Polyfilla was *not* a good idea was it? You should have read the instructions on the box before you indulged your naughty D.I.Y. whims.

And finally:

Bob of Bobbing... No, I would not recommend a lawn mower — even with a safety cut-out device. A hair dryer would be much more sensible. Or, failing that you can't go wrong with a nice reliable Teasmaid.

Mrs McTavish,

Maih husband and Aih request one shoulder to cry on as ones children really are a burden and a continuous cause for concern.

Ones eldest son constantly falls orf horses and talks to plants, while ones daughter only talks to horses.

Ones middle son ran orf to sea many years ago after dalliance with a succession of beautiful gels.

But ones biggest worry is the youngest son who was tragically made redundant just as his career in showbusiness looked so promising. He was about to be promoted from sweeping the stage and clearing the empty ice cream cartons from the aisles, to the

responsible and elevated position of Acting Departmental Coffee &
Sticky Bun Distributor.

It has helped to know one so experienced and caring as yourself,
Flora (One may call you Flora?), is on hand with a sympathic ear.

LIZ and PHIL

Dear Flora,

I fear my husband has fallen under the spell of a scheming, steaming vamp.

He is a school teacher, a quiet, unassuming man whose only vice is a medium-sweet sherry once a week at the Upper Budleigh Budgies' Breeding Brotherhood Hall.

But, frankly Flora, I am a very worried woman since hearing a snatch of conversation while pondering over the pigs' livers last week in the Supermarket.

Two of the Dinner Ladies from my husband's school canteen were talking (I knew who they were from their funny white caps and the gravy down the front of their pinnies). To my horror I heard them say that *my husband* just couldn't stay away from that Gypsy Tart... he couldn't get enough and his appetite was insatiable.

Oh! Flora... I can just imagine that Gypsy tart with her flashing gold earrings bedazzling my poor innocent Harold. Clacking her castanets under his cute little turned-up nose and confusing his senses with a hot-blooded Fandango and a swirl of red silk petticoat.

How can I possibly save him from the clutches of this rampant Romany?

My only hope is that I have misunderstood the situation.

'UPSET' OF UPPER BUDLEIGH

54

Black Toe Knee Burn

The Mid Morning Muddle is nothing if not controversial.

In a misguided moment (or it could have been a recurrence of his 'old trouble') Marshy played the Tony Blackburn song. You must remember it, it goes Tony Blackburn, Tony Blackburn, Tony Blackburn, Tony Blackburn... then it goes Tony Blackburn, Tony Blackburn, Tony Blackburn... Ah! yes, it's all coming back now isn't it?

It brought a flood of letters.

And they were all threatening.

'If he plays that record again I will have him put out to grass with the lions at Howlett's Zoo Park wearing Barbara Sturgeon's fishnet tights only — or perhaps a day locked in my bubble car with the windows closed,' wrote someone called Fred.

'If you play that record again Pat, then I will post this letter without a stamp,' John Palmer, Rochester.

Then there was an unsigned letter from the 'Association of Medway Godfathers'. It asked, most politely, for the playing of the record to cease forthwith or the boys would pay a visit with a pair of concrete shoes. The Association was most thoughtful in its choice of location for Marsh's little dip. They chose the Medway just off the Sun Pier so that he could be near his place of work.

Thank goodness he stopped playing it. There is enough pollution in the Medway as it is.

All In A Lather

There is always something exciting happening at the Oast.

Do you remember the time when the Station Manager was having a jacuzzi installed in his Private Suite?

The news broke on the Mid Morning Show and everyone followed the saga with great interest. Regulars were full of helpful advice.

Dear Pat,

I feel I must join in the Great Jacuzzi Debate. I have listened to you all getting extremely excited and steamed up just because the thing is stuck in the lift.

The answer is simple — you leave it in the lift, stock up with a few plastic ducks and a couple of gallons of bubble bath, and you will be the envy of every Radio Station in the vicinity.

The basic idea is — every time you go up or down in the lift you can have a jacuzzi at the same time.

There will, of course, have to be a set of rules and regulations; like no more than eight people standing at any one time. And Management to have exclusive use of the loofah on Mondays and Thursdays.

Large plastic ducks and wind-up torpedoes will be available by filling in an application form and handing to the Reception Desk three days prior to requirement. *Small* plastic ducks and empty Squeezy bottles (I personally find these give me hours of fun on a Friday night) will be available on 1 hour's notice.

Of course, like everything else in this world, the hoity-toity will have preferential treatment at all times. Technically speaking, this means those with the biggest increments get the most jacuzzies.

The eating of cream crackers will be strictly forbidden, and if you must do the Times crossword — please ensure it is not left all limp and soggy for the next occupant.

The benefits of this scheme are immediately apparent. Think of the next time Mo Meadows comes calling. After parking his muck-spreader in the car park he can pop straight into the lift (boots an' all) and by the time he reaches you he will be smelling as sweet as a freshly harvested turnip.

If Radio ever catches on and regular listeners reach double figures, then perhaps some of the profits could be invested in a sauna for the other lift.

And in the future, who knows, a massage parlour in the third lift.

Sing-Along-A Work

Some songs seem to be custom made for certain occupations. Here are a few to get you humming:

SEWER OPERATIVE	I Should Be So Mucky — Kylie Minogue
MARKET TRADER	Chirpy, Chirpy, Cheap, Cheap.
RECORD SALESMAN	Like A Virgin
EGYPTOLOGIST	I Sphinx I Love You
DERMATOLOGIST	I've Got You Under My Skin
LINGERIE SALESMAN	Strangers In The Nightie
DENTIST	Driller — Michael Jackson
BUTCHER	We'll Meat Again
WINDOW CLEANER	The Clean, Clean Glass Of Home — Tom Jones
YACHTSMAN	Mad About The Buoy
CHEF	Love Letters Straight From The Tart
SEWER FARM WORKER	Whose Slurry Now — Connie Francis
PAINTER & DECORATOR	I Second That Emulsion — Smokey Robinson & The Miracles

Then, of course, some people could have their own personal signature tune.

Frankenstein's Monster — Put Your Head On My Shoulder
Mick Jagger — Tip-Toe Through The Two Lips
Glenys Kinnock — Lady In Red
John Major — Fade To Grey
Paddy Ashdown — For All The Girls I've Loved Before
Cliff Richard — Goody Two Shoes
Ronnie Corbett — Little Things Mean A Lot
Joan Collins — I Like It
Michael Fish — The Sun Ain't Gonna Shine Any More
Barbara Sturgeon — She's Gone
Dave Austin — I Wanna Wake Up With You
Elizabeth Taylor — I'm Getting Married In The Morning

What's Happened To Auntie Nellie?

What's happened to Auntie Nellie?
I'd really like to know.
Has she gone off with a toy boy
Sunning it up on the Costa Del Sol?
Now she's abandoned her corsets,
Letting it all hang free;
Has she changed her lifestyle
For one of iniquity?
My mind began to boggle
Until I heard the news.
The poor soul's gone to Switzerland
Taking in mountain views.
No doubt she's on a ski run,
Standing on a piste.
Forgetting just how old she is
As she puts her life at risk.
Perhaps she'll meet a man at last,
Someone rather nice
Who will put some romance into her life
With a bunch of Edelweiss.
Enjoy yourself, Aunt Nellie,
Come back safe and sound,
'Cos 'Silver Award' Marshy
Likes having you around.

Rosemary Huckerby, Maidstone

And thus began one of the greatest mysteries the world has ever known.

Not since the wheels of Marshy's Robin Reliant were nicked has there been such uproar at the Oast. They were never found. In fact, it was three weeks before Pat realised they were missing, and he never bothered to report it to the Police because the Robin ran more smoothly without them anyway.

But to return to the enigma that was Auntie Nellie.

One minute she was there — the next...gone! With only a half finished cup of Horlicks and a pair of still-warm headphones to indicate that she even existed.

There were many reported sightings, all sadly mistaken identities. Many organised searches, all fruitless. And much concern from all MMMs.

Fabian Dowker, the Mad Scientist of Singlewell, had a theory that it was Auntie Nellie making all the corn circles that were hitting the headlines at the time. He was of the opinion (having run one of his Rigid Practical Tests) that she had taken up breeding glow-worms and saw-fleas, which feed on corn stalks at night.

He also swears, in a subsequent letter, that he got through to the switchboard and recognised the answering voice as that of Aunt Nellie.

'Like a reversal of the theme in "Charley's Aunt" (who had to be present when not actually there) I think Auntie Nellie is pretending *not* to be present when she really is. You have created a sort of phantom kidnapping so I am ceasing my search for Auntie Nellie and calling off the Hounds of the Basketballs.'

Some listeners had their own ideas about the situation...

> Poor Nellie was blue
> (With good reason, it's true)
> As she worked hard while Pat played the clown.
> She was angry because
> He got all the applause,
> And it finally wore Nellie down.
>
> So she chucked the job in
> And now Pat's in a spin,
> As there's no clue to where Nellie's gone.
> Now he struggles alone
> To answer the phone
> And get the Mid Morning Show on.
>
> He has had to confess
> That the place is a mess.
> And he's up to his eyeballs in mail.
> That as sure as hell, he
> Will have to find Nellie;
> Tho' his efforts are destined to fail.
>
> For tho' rumours abound —
> To confuse and confound
> Is their patently obvious purpose,
> As he heard it's a fact
> That Aunt Nellie has packed
> And has upped and away to the Circus.

Now the moral, Pat dear,
Is perfectly clear,
If you don't want your Staff to defect.
Give credit where due and
Whatever you do,
Treat elders with love and respect!

Carol Banks
Sheerness

Then... shock, horror... a ransom demand.

Pat

AUNTIE NELLY IS
OK FOR NOW

NO POLICE KGB
CIA SAS OR TUFTY
CLUB — TWO
THOUSAND GOODIE BAGS
OR CURTAINS FOR HER
SPANISH POSTAL GANG

Two thousand Goodie Bags, it said. But failed to mention whether the Mid Morning Programme was to leave them for the kidnappers — or whether they had been 'won' by unfortunate listeners who were anxious to hand them back to Radio Kent.

It also stated 'or curtains for her' which everyone thought was a jolly good swap. Mrs McTavish had a measure up and a general concensus around the Studio decided that something in Dusky Pink velveteen would be nice. But although a note was left giving the size of the window and the style of tie-backs chosen — nothing was forthcoming from the Spanish Postal Gang.

So there it ended.

No more has been heard of Auntie Nellie, and Mrs McTavish took over her desk, finished her Horlicks, and remains to this day.

In Memoriam

Aunt Nellie was not the only one to disappear without trace over the last few years.

Remember Marmaduke the cat? Rumour has it that Marshy had him spirited away because he was receiving more fan mail than himself.

And the Weather Girls were made redundant because, as Pat explained, Kent was not going to have any more weather due to lack of interest. A likely story!

They staged a mass walkout because of Sexual Harrassment — there wasn't any...

Truth is, Marshy refused to sew the sequins on their thermal bustiers any more — so they high-kicked their way to Italy where you can get your bottom pinched every day for free and you can wear fishnet stockings without the goose pimples getting hooked up in the mesh.

Chateau Chaos

Dear Pat,

It may not have escaped your notice that lately you have not received any news of Old Uncle Joe.

I may as well take the bull by the horns and 'butter no parsnips' as he would say, and reveal that at the moment he no longer resides at Chateau Chaos. He mysteriously moved out some weeks ago, not long after spending his holiday at Gravesend.

Not being one to think that 'The darkest hour is paved with good intentions', I must say that he moved out not long after your very own Auntie Nellie went missing. Not that I am saying there is anything in the local rumour that Old Uncle Joe may be involved with a woman of 'super star' status; but you must admit that *sometimes* there is no smoke if it's five before eleven!

I don't personally believe that Old Uncle Joe and your Auntie Nellie are together. Anyhow, he is not romantic enough for her. When we claimed that 'matches are made in Heaven' he said 'Surely they are made in Sweden'.

I am rather worried about Old Uncle Joe, as he is not in the best of health. Only yesterday I read a report that said the wearing of tight clothes can affect the circulation; and I remember once he saw a girl wearing jeans so tight that he could hardly breathe.

You may have heard that he is a bit of a dude, but he really has been through the Mill. He is what you call 'Mildewed'.

If I hear any definite news I shall let you know.

Don't worry about Aunt Nellie — better an old man's darling than a young man's slave!

Alan the Alien
alias
Alan Stephens,
Limpsfield Chart

You Know You Are Getting Old

When...

The toys you played with as a child now appear with alarming frequency on the Antiques Road Show.

Chelsea Pensioners look young.

You can remember buying Cliff Richard's first record.

The medicine cabinet has more in it than the fridge.

You look in the mirror and your mother/father's face is looking back at you.

You sit in the rocking chair... and you can't get it started.

Men reach the awful conclusion when the bald patch at the front of their head meets the bald patch coming the other way from the back of their head.
    And ladies... no hope for you, I fear, when you look on Mel Gibson as 'just another actor'.

Further warning signs to look for are...

You don't know who the bands are on Top of the Pops
You are going to bed just as the children are going out
A zimmer frame looks quite attractive
You think a microchip is a small fried potato
Boy Scouts rush to help you at Zebra Crossings
You never leave the house without your cardi
You think Max Bygraves is an alternative comedian
Your teeth are out more often than you are
You buy your first pair of slippers
You have to mash everything you eat

From Bad to Verse . . . a further selection of poems

JUMBLE SALES

Jumble sale!
Super, great.
My idea of heaven.

Church Hall
School Gate.
Waiting for 11.00.

Chin up
Elbows out
Ready to stampede.

First in
Charge ahead.
Lots of things I need.

Grab this,
Sort that.
Find myself a patch.

Mauve scarf,
Pink hat.
Do you think they match?

One glove,
Dolls legs,
Amazing what you find.

Tatty books,
Clothes pegs,
Madam!... do you mind.

Stony glare,
Quick tug,
You can't be too polite.

Brand new
Hearth rug.
(Surely worth a fight)

Battered ribs,
Squashed toe,
Bargains by the score.

Bruised shins,
Even so,
I'll be back for more.

Battle scarred
Tuckered out.
Like a wilted flower.

But proud to say,
As Churchill did.
'This was my finest hour'.

DON'T TOUCH

Mummy took me shopping.
I love it oh, so much.
Mummy warned me 'Tarquin,
Don't touch'.

We visited the toy shop.
My eyes lit up with glee.
I grabbed — and fifty teddies
Buried me.

Then we went to Tesco's
and with a nervous cough
Mummy pleaded 'Tarquin,
Hands off'.

Sneaking past the tinned food
Mummy's being very brave.
A hiss through clenched teeth threatened
'Behave'.

Isn't it amazing
How far a totem pole
Of neatly piled baked bean tins
Can roll!

Five hundred packs of cornflakes
Stacked in a pyramid.
They say you can't move mountains.
I did!

Is it time for home already?
There's much more yet to see.
Tell me Mummy that you truly
Still love me...

HOUSEWIFE'S CHOICE

It happens in the morning
Every week-day without fail.
Starting at 9.30
Come sunshine, rain or hail.

It keeps us from the hoovering,
Our dusters we abandon.
We down all tools and twiddle knobs
'Till Radio Kent we land on.

No time to stop and feed the cat
Or change the baby's nappy.
We have to take our daily dose
Of Marsh to keep us happy.

Now if you have a problem,
If your hubby won't or can't.
Then Flora has the answer —
She's our resident Agony Aunt.

At Wendy's house the family
All keep her on her toes.
And what that man-mad Beryl's up to
Heaven only knows.

Our Rosie Beer's the lady
Whose poems we adore.
Her quirky slant on life
Will have you rolling on the floor.

Mo Meadows comes to spread the word
Straight from his cattle sheds.
But 'cos he never wipes his feet
That isn't all he spreads.

And rumour has it, Marshy,
As he drives his cart along,
Stores close up and shoppers faint.
Could it be the pong?

With its quizzes, games and letters
With its loadsa laughs and fun,
The old Mid Morning Muddle
Is the housewives' No. 1.

BED AND BORED

Lying in your sickbed,
As everybody knows,
Is so out and out dead boring
That I thought I'd count my toes.
But when I'd counted up to ten
And I couldn't make it more,
I thought perhaps, I'd count the
Marley tiles on the floor.
But when I'd counted eighty-three
And my eyes began to spin,
I thought I'd count the bedpans
As Nursie wheeled them in.
And then I counted all the teeth
A-nestling in my glass.
Then all the grapes left in the dish
Another hour to pass.
At last it's time for dinner.
Make it my favourite please.
'Cos if it's fish and chips today
Then I can count the peas..

The Old Robin Reliant

I have already touched on the subject of the Robin Reliant. It's Pat's pride and joy. He can be very touchy should anyone cast aspersions on its reliability or social standing. It is polished lovingly with a ginger fur mitt (oh! no! Marmaduke?) and should it rain then lowly members of the Oast are despatched in rotation to throw themselves across the Robin thus preserving the paintwork.

This flurry of fluorescent yellow paintwork can be seen roaring from the Oast car park at 11.31 a.m. every weekday, with the speed of a canary being sucked up the Hoover.

Unfortunately, beauty is in the eye of the beholder, and not everyone regards it with the same reverence as Marshy.

When he left it parked outside his house on one occasion he was most upset to find a note under the windscreen wiper threatening that the dumping of rubbish on the Highway was an offence punishable by a fine or imprisonment, or both.

But, at least, it is recognised wherever it goes.

Little old ladies feel safe on Pelican Crossings (in fact, little old tortoises feel safe on Pelican Crossings).

72

Cyclists wave cheerily as they overtake, taking care to slow down so as not to cause a slipstream.

And there is no truth in the rumour that it is only the string on the seat covers that is holding it together.

The MMM's are a helpful lot, and I suppose Jean Pope of Queenborough thought Pat might find the following useful...

How to dismantle engine in ten easy lessons

LESSON 1

Take spanner in right hand — or left if you are left-handed (if you have no hands then it might be advisable to see a chiropodist).

LESSON 2

Take screwdriver and screw to the left — or is it to the right? It depends if you are Labour or Conservative. If you are in labour then call out the midwife. If you are Conservative then you are turning blue and should go indoors and put on some warmer clothing.

LESSON 3

On releasing the screw you will find a metal plate shaped like a horse shoe. This could mean you have been driving over the Sheppey Bridge while it was 'up', or the woman standing in the road wearing jodhpurs and waving a riding crop furiously was trying to relay a message regarding her horse.

LESSON 4

When metal plate is removed you will find four holes. Do not worry. They are there to confuse you. Just find three other people, put one finger in one hole and the three other people each put a finger in the other holes. Just say 'One, two, three, lift', and out it comes.

LESSON 5

Now revealed are hundreds of nuts and bolts. Don't worry. You have three other people there who will not be leaving...mainly because they cannot remove their fingers from the holes. So while you wait for the Fire Brigade give them a spanner each, and with their remaining hand they can loosen as many screws and nuts as they can reach.

LESSON 6

Give Fire Brigade and the three captive assistants a cup of tea. By now the engine should be very loose and ready to lift out. Why not ask the Fire Officer if you can use his hoist as he is handy?

LESSON 7

Slide a fireman under the car with a rope, with instructions to hold wobbly Jack with one hand and tie a knot in the rope with the other. The rest of you can just stand around and have a good laugh.

LESSON 8

Shout 'lift' and the engine should rise effortlessly. If you should hear screaming at this stage don't panic, it is probably the fireman underneath holding wobbly Jack. Anyway, no one asked Jack for his help. You cannot be held responsible for his misfortunes.

LESSON 9

You have done very well so far and have not spilt a single drop of oil. This is probably because there was none in there in the first place.

LESSON 10

There we are then…one engine removed from car, and it didn't take long thanks to the Fire Brigade, three people with their fingers still stuck firmly in the holes and not forgetting wobbly Jack (he really should have stuck to that diet).

Little Jack Horner
Sat in the corner
Eating his TV dinner.
He said 'what a cheat,
There'll be nothing to eat
If this pizza base gets any thinner.'

The Twaddle Party

When Election Fever hits the country, Radio Kent listeners work themselves up to a frenzy of zealous campaigning...Marshy for Prime Minister...etc....

Many suggestions were forthcoming for a title for the Mid-Morning Muddle Political Party.

The 'Bring a Bottle Party', the 'All Night Party', and even the 'Lingerie Party', but Twaddle Party seemed the most appropriate... and so it was named.

Ever mindful of the financial side of politics the Twaddle Tours Moped and Trolley Runs Society was formed. The basic principle being to link together a train of supermarket trollies, hitch them to Mo Meadow's muck spreader (empty, of course) and conduct parties of Japanese and American tourists round the more interesting and cultural parts of Kent.

Steve Bodington of Gravesend, alias the Mad Mopeder, one of the Twaddle Party's most staunch supporters, wrote:

'Here at the Twaddle Tours Moped and Trolley Runs Society, we have been working three hundred and sixty-five days a week for seven days a year. Many of the Trolley Run staff have been working fifty-two hours a day in order to maintain the extremely poor level of comfort and reliability that our customers know can only come from us.

'It is also the hard work and back-breaking effort which our team have become accustomed to providing that has kept us on our peak form for competitive prices. However, Twaddle Tours hereby give warning that in the near future we will have to up prices by 3% in order to make an extra few pence per week to feed our new break-down service. His name is "Texas Timothy", and he is a five-legged horse we have had imported from the USA at great expense and inconvenience to ourselves.'

He went on to say:

'Unfortunately, Trolley Tours made a loss of four pence last year (a deficit which I hope will be rectified this year).

'There is a ray of hope however. Our trade deficit is only to be short lived as we are one of those companies that are making money from the recent spell of wet weather.

'It is a new advance in trolley travel, our engineers have crossed a baby's pram with a supermarket trolley and have come up with a sort of Cabriolet version.

'This allows the passengers to pull up a kind of baby's pram type hood, to shelter from whatever the weather has to throw at them. And I can reveal exclusively to the Mid-Morning Show that we have also managed to incorporate a type of electric window into the side of the hood, so that the American and Japanese tourists can take photos in the trolley without getting wet.'

Should the tourist trade drop off for any reason, there were other suggestions for the use of the "trolley-train". From the Mad Mopeder again:

'You may remember that a kind listener offered the services of her German cousin, Herr Pinbend. (This was for the purpose of building a new tunnel connecting the Isle of Sheppey with the rest of Europe). Well, I took my fifteen trolleys to Sheerness to take the rubble away, and even took my own dessert spoon along to assist the afore-mentioned Herr Pinbend in his efforts in the "Twunnell".' (the name given to the new Twaddle Tunnel).

There was an appeal for old cans and bits of string in order to build a communication system for the Twaddle Headquarters, and the offer of accommodation. Actually it was a disused Portaloo (luxury model, with windows and 'engaged' sign).

Well at least the Party leaders could meet in comfort and 'pass a motion'. *And* there would be plenty of paper for the Secretary to take Minutes.

One of the main aims of the Twaddle Party was Independence for the Isle of Sheppey. The idea was, under the cover of darkness or taking advantage of the murky fog that envelopes Sheppey most winter evenings, specially-trained Commandoes would storm the Kingsferry Bridge. Loosening certain strategic nuts and bolts, the Island could be pushed gently out to sea away from the mainland and (hopefully) float lazily off to sunnier climes.

The natives were all for it. And at the time it seemed a better proposition than the 'Twunnell'. At least, that was the cunning plan of Mathew Irving of Sheerness.

'I've always fancied a world cruise,' he wrote. 'We would miss Radio Kent of course, but if a satellite connection was arranged — our trip would be perfect. When election time comes round once again I shall write to all the parties (including the one that goes on all night at No. 73) about this — but I am sure the Twaddle Party is the one I can rely on.'

Unfortunately, despite all the rumours, Marshy does not have a large majority. The Twaddle Party never made it that time round and Sheerness with its adjoining areas, Shepponions and sheep, was still there last time I looked.

Job Lot

I thought of taking a job in the garden centre — but there wasn't any fuschia in it.

The job I really wanted as a Medium just did not materialise, and there was a job sharpening pencils — but I didn't see the point of that at all.

I even tried working in the fishmongers — but I couldn't stand the plaice.

Then for a time I worked in a gents' outfitters — but it didn't suit me.

I did not come up to scratch at the flea circus, and the Channel Tunnel was boring.

Then I had a spell as a magician, got cheesed-off at the Dairy and could not stick the job of bill poster.

Postbox

An odd assortment of letters — from an odd assortment of listeners.

Dear Pat,

Don't some people have strange hobbies.

There was great excitement at Gillingham the other day when word went round there was a strange foreign bird perched up a tree (no... it was not a Swedish stripper blown off-course while migrating).

Apparently, it was a three legged, lesser spotted, greeble warbler ... or some such thing.

'Twitchers' (bird watchers) came flooding in from all directions with their cameras and binoculars to gawp, enthralled by the sight.

Personally, I could not see what all the fuss was about. Now if it had been a well-oiled, lesser clothed Chippendale, well — I could understand it. In fact, I would have been the first in the queue with my binoculars 'twitching' away for all I was worth.

No...my hobby is much more sedate. Building model ships in bottles. Well, er... I have not actually built one yet. I am still in the initial stage, which involves emptying the bottles. Another couple of years and I might be ready to start on my first project.

Actually, my first attempt was a bit of a disaster. It was supposed to be the QE2 — but no one told me you are supposed to empty the bottle first — so to save embarrassment I hastily re-christened it the Titanic.

Dear Pat,

There has been great media interest lately regarding the most speedy and efficient way to lose weight.

The arguments for and against are many. But let me issue some dire warnings to those foolhardy enough to be tempted by these new-fangled remedies currently in vogue.

Firstly, the process whereby the stomach is stapled, making it smaller and thus reducing its capacity for food intake.

My friend tried this.

Being a very modest young lady she insisted on keeping her night-gown on during the operation; as a result of which she found herself firmly stapled to her nightie and it was three weeks before she could get it off to go shopping.

Liposuction is another method to be approached with the greatest of caution. In this, the fat is sucked from the offending areas with tubes. But, be warned, another of my friends (6 ft tall and built like a Sumo wrestler) tried liposuction some years ago, while it was still in its experimental stage.

Tragically, the surgeon was inexperienced, sucked too hard — and now she is only 4 ft 3 ins.

The moral of this story must be 'Don't dabble with the flab'.

Dear Marshy,

Your secret is out. You are not the bright and breezy sophisticated man you appear to be.

I know the truth.

You are shunned by everybody at Radio Kent aren't you?

You shuffle in through the tradesmen's entrance in the morning to your seat which they cover with old newspapers just before you arrive. They are ashamed of you and your muddly show. After all, they bring a little culture to Radio Kent. What, I ask you Marshy, do you bring? Apart from a load of twaddle.

Even the tea lady peers through the glass in disgust at you and refuses to bring your morning coffee in. You sit there in your finger-less gloves with blue nose dripping onto the turntable — ears red under your peaked cap, feet clad in ancient carpet slippers, and a six-foot scarf wound round and round your neck so that only a pair of bleak bloodshot eyes can be seen peering out at the world.

You reach down into your old brown carrier bag for your Thermos flask and slice of bread and dripping.

I know, Marshy, I know!

At 11.30 a.m. you sadly put on your old pac-a-mac and shuffle backwards out of the door. Even the Producer averts his eyes when you pass him on the way out.

You then hobble off down Chatham High Street, talking to yourself in the hope that someone will recognise your voice and ask for your autograph.

You then go into the Rat and Handbag for a Milk Stout before making your way home to your lonely damp-ridden, rat infested bed-sit, where you sit warming your hands over the single gas ring.

You then start writing letters to yourself and posting them to Radio Kent making out they are from listeners, when you really know there are none.

And, finally, the guests you make out you have on your show.

Own up, Marshy. There are no guests. You have, in desperation, learnt the art of mimicry. You do it very well. Although you did not have David Essex's voice quite right.

Marilyn Reynolds
Broadstairs.

Just to keep you up to date with my 'Helium Knickers' Atlantic race with Richard Branson.

Well, I have had a bit of a set-back.

As I haven't actually got a map, I had the bright idea of tracing the Thames by putting my tracing paper over the opening titles for 'Eastenders'. It gives a lovely clear map of the River and surrounding areas.

Somewhere I must have gone wrong, Pat. I jumped gaily off the Tower Bridge to cheering crowds (well, two small children) and clutching my 'map' I floated along until I suddenly realised I was over my own road in Gravesend. I had gone and copied the 'D' in Eastenders as part of the map.

Looking down, I saw our old friend The Mad Mopeder, head down with a trolley load of tourists.

Could you ask him, Marshy, to give me a wave next time I zoom over? I could even arrange a very cheap return flight to America for his tourists.

Pauline,
Gravesend.

Doggone

If, like the Mid Morning Muddle, you have gone to the dogs, then you should be able to put a name to these famous pooches — fact and fiction...

1. Dorothy's companion in the Wizard of Oz.

2. A shaggy heroine, who was in fact male, and one of the few who actually kissed Elizabeth Taylor without ending up married to her.

3. The Super-Snooper who found the stolen F.A. Cup in a front garden.

4. Pictured listening intently to the sound issuing from a very early gramophone record. Lucky for him he was not around to listen to the Mid Morning Muddle.

5. Little white dog (a clue here) belonging to cartoon character Tin-Tin.

6. Bassett hound cartoon strip dog.

7. Another cartoon strip hound with some very strange friends — including a small bird.

8. This cartoon dawg (I am being over-generous with clues here) carries a gun and wears a badge.

9. Take a trip to Euro-Disney and you are bound to run into him and his pal Mickey.

10. Twist my arm and I'll give you the Dickens of a clue to the identity of this ugly dog with the little short legs and a patch over one eye.

ANSWERS:

10. Bullseye.
6. Fred Bassett. 7. Snoopy. 8. Deputy Dawg. 9. Pluto.
1. Toto. 2. Lassie. 3. Pickles. 4. Nipper. 5. Snowy.

Things You Don't Do With Newspaper Any More

1. Cut it into six inch squares, thread string through the corner and hang in the smallest room.

2. Lay it on the floor under the lino.

3. Wrap fish and chips.

4. Use a double page held over the fire surround, to draw a draught up the chimney and get the coal going.

5. Line the bottom of the drawers in the tallboy.

6. Fold into the shape of a boat, and sail it in the gutter to amuse the kids.

Up the Poll

When the nation was first threatened with the dreaded Poll Tax, Pat Marsh was very confident that he could avoid paying by throwing all the poles in his back garden over next door's fence.

Poor misguided, innocent lad.

He was wracked with worries that Captain Kent and the one-legged tramp might be taxed on their wooden legs.

He fretted over Mrs McTavish, thinking she might be forced to give up her beloved hobby of tossing the caber (which she can be seen practising religiously every lunch hour at the end of the Sun Pier).

The following missive set him straight:

Trust you Marshy! You have got the wrong end of the stick (or should that be pole).

It's POLL Tax — not POLE Tax!

If you look in your Concise Oxford Dictionary (page 794) you will read: POLL — PARROT: Tame Parrot.

Therefore, anyone with a bird that resembles an oversize budgie; that swears and eats Brazil nuts, will be liable to cough up this new fangled Tax. (Spooky — that could be a description of my Aunt Dolly.)

Captain Kent springs to mind. He peg-legs it round Kent burying his treasure in obscure villages, with his parrot on one shoulder and shovel on the other. No way can he avoid the Poll Tax. His dry cleaning bill for jackets alone will bear testament to the fact that he totes a parrot around all day.

And all those football managers who are 'as sick as parrots' will have to pay up as well — or find a new expression.

How about 'sick as an Aardvark'?

POLL vaulting will become a rich man's sport, and POLL-o players, the POLL-ice and all POLL-ish nationals will be liable.

POLL-ar bears and POLL-cats will eventually cost too much for the average householder to keep as pets, and the price of POLL-aroid cameras will rocket.

Personally, I think it's a load of old POLL-ock (marine food fish of genus Pollachius, allied to cod, but with protruding lower jaw).

Mary, Mary, quite contrary,
How does your garden grow?
Well, since I have follard
Advice from Bob Collard
I've won first prize in every big show!

And finally, no book would be complete without a look into the future.

So here it is...

Old Marsh's Almanac

January

I predict that this will be the first month of the New Year. There will be a great deal of inactivity in the first two weeks, and sales of paracatemol will rocket.

February

Lots of weather this month. In fact, right through the month.

February will see a great deal of unrest at the Radio Kent studio. The inmates will turn ugly (though it is difficult to imagine some of them any more ugly than they already are) as heated debates reach boiling point over the malfunctioning of the hot drinks dispenser.

March

Expect to see developments in the hot drinks dispenser saga. Riots ensue when the Studio Head explains that the tomato soup, that looks like tea and tastes like cocoa, is in fact coffee.

April

In the Grand National, put your money on a brown horse with a leg at each corner.

A combination of heavy April showers and a build-up of surplus water due to the continuous hosepipe ban, will result in the flooding of the River Medway. The Radio Kent Oast House will be swept away on rising tides and disappear out to sea.

Broadcasts, however, will continue uninterrupted.

May

The world will be shocked when Michael Jackson sneezes violently and disintegrates into a pile of spare parts. There will be a short period of mourning while someone rushes for a dustpan and brush.

June

Sightings are reported of the Oast bobbing around just South of Zanzibar.

There will also be unfounded rumours that the Isle of Sheppey is not far behind, with the Natives astride what remains of the Kings Ferry Bridge, paddling furiously to catch up.

July

Lots of people eating ice cream, wearing shorts, mowing lawns and sitting on beaches.

Sales of flip-flops will be up.

August

Lots of people eating curled up sandwiches, wearing shorts, not mowing lawns and sitting in Airport Lounges.

Sales of air sick-bags will be up.

September

Oast reported rounding the Northern-most tip of Australia. The dispute regarding the tea machine will be forgotten as staff live off coconut milk and bananas.

October

In the first few days of the month I predict tidal waves, earthquakes, avalanches, volcanic eruptions and landslides. In fact, quite an eventful week in Chatham High Street.

My advice would be to stay indoors and don't go to Tesco's until at least Thursday.

November

Scandal breaks when Mrs McTavish elopes with Mo Meadows.

Investigations reveal Lord Lucan and Elvis working as farmhands for Mo, for the last two years Aunt Nellie and Uncle Joe have been housekeeper and butler, and Shergar has been pulling Mo's muckspreader around the farm.

December

The Radio Kent Oast finally comes to rest, ties up to the nearest Banyan tree and is re-named Radio Bahamas.

Whatever you do — stay tuned for another year of the best in entertainment and the most fun you can have without being arrested...

Our special thanks to the following friends of the Mid Morning Mob who have unwittingly endangered their careers by appearing on the show . . .

David Essex
Gene Pitney
Status Quo
Sacha Distel
LaToya Jackson
Rick Wakeman
Dr Hook
Nigel Kennedy
Howard Keel
Barbara Dickson
Chesney Hawkes
Kenny Ball
Daniel O'Donnel
Rose Marie
Alan Price
Chas n' Dave
Johnny Logan
Bucks Fizz
The Barron Knights
The Searchers
The Seekers
Petula Clarke
Jerry & The Pacemakers
Freddie & The Dreamers
Paul Jones
Harold Melvin
Ruby Turner
Richard Clayderman
Vince Hill
Mud
Peters & Lee
Alvin Stardust
Showaddywaddy
Suzie Quatro
Jermaine Jackson
Foster and Alan
The Flying Pickets

Roger Whittaker
Rolf Harris
Frankie Vaughan
Anthony Newley
Val Doonican
Keith Harris & Orville
Brendan Shine
Des O'Connor
Ken Dodd
Gary Wilmott
Patrick Moore
Raymond Baxter
Patrick Mower
Leslie Crowther
Jackie Collins
Ruth Madoc
Gordon Kaye
Sue Pollard
Paul Nicholas
Simon Ward
Paul Shane
Barbara Windsor
Jimmy Jones
Jackie Pallo
Max Boyce
Phil Cool
Mike Harding
Roy Hudd
Danny La Rue
Donald Sinden
Frank Muir
Michael Bentine
Harry Secombe
Norman Wisdom
Rory Bremner
Max Bygraves
Henry Kelly

Jimmy Cricket
Paul Daniels
Wayne Sleep
Bobby Davro
Russell Grant
Jessica Martin
Ronnie Corbett
Cannon and Ball
Wayne Dobson
The Beverley Sisters
Anita Harris
Tim Rice
Lenny Henry
Tony Slattery
Suzanne Dando
Johnny Morris
Rod, Jane & Freddie
Peter Davidson
Sandra Dickson

Mark Curry
Colin Baker
Sooty
Tony Hart
Jeff Banks
Wendy Richard
Helen Worth
Barry McGuigan
Terry Marsh
Gary Mason
Jan Leeming
Bill Giles
Frances Wilson
Michael Fish
John Kettley
Ron Lobeck
Michael Van Straten
Dr Mike Smith
Dr Hilary Jones

. . . Backword

So there you are... thank you to everyone who has joined in the Mid Morning Show and made this book what it is.

A load of twaddle.

If you'd like to be a part of the next one you're always welcome to join us on any weekday morning.

We're waiting to hear from you...!

Meresborough Books

17 Station Road, Rainham, Gillingham, Kent. ME8 7RS
Telephone: Medway (0634) 388812

We are a specialist publisher of books about Kent. Our books are available in most bookshops in the county, including our own at this address. Alternatively you may order direct, adding 10% for post (minimum 50p, orders over £30 post free). ISBN prefix 0 905270 for 3 figure numbers, 094819 for 4 figure numbers. Titles in print December 1992.

HARDBACKS

AIRCRAFT CASUALTIES IN KENT Part One 1939-40 compiled by G.G. Baxter, K.A. Owen and P. Baldock. ISBN 3506. £12.95.

BARGEBUILDING ON THE SWALE by Don Sattin. ISBN 3530. £9.95.

EDWARDIAN CHISLEHURST by Arthur Battle. ISBN 3433. £9.95.

FISHERMEN FROM THE KENTISH SHORE by Derek Coombe. ISBN 3409. £10.95.

THE HISTORY OF THE ROYAL SEA BATHING HOSPITAL, MARGATE 1791-1991 by F.G. St Clair Strange. ISBN 3573. £12.95.

JUST OFF THE SWALE by Don Sattin. ISBN 045. £5.95.

KENT: A PORTRAIT IN COLOUR by John Guy. ISBN 3700. £12.95.

KENT'S OWN by Robin J. Brooks. The history of 500 (County of Kent) Squadron of the R.A.A.F. ISBN 541. £5.95.

THE LONDON, CHATHAM & DOVER RAILWAY by Adrian Gray. ISBN 886. £7.95.

A NEW DICTIONARY OF KENT DIALECT by Alan Major. ISBN 274. £7.50.

THE PAST GLORY OF MILTON CREEK by Alan Cordell and Leslie Williams. ISBN 3042. £9.95.

THE PLACE NAMES OF KENT by Judith Glover. ISBN 614. £7.50. BARGAIN OFFER £4.95.

ROCHESTER FROM OLD PHOTOGRAPHS compiled by the City of Rochester Society. Large format. ISBN 975. £7.95.(Also available in paperback ISBN 983. £4.95.)

SHERLOCK HOLMES AND THE KENT RAILWAYS by Kelvin Jones. ISBN 3255. £8.95.

A SIDEWAYS LAUNCH by Anne Salmon. ISBN 3689. £15.95.

STRATFORD HOUSE SCHOOL 1912-1987 by Susan Pittman. ISBN 3212. £10.00.

TALES OF VICTORIAN HEADCORN or The Oddities of Heddington by Penelope Rivers (Ellen M. Poole). ISBN 3050. £8.95. (Also available in paperback ISBN 3069. £3.95).

TEYNHAM MANOR AND HUNDRED (798-1935) by Elizabeth Selby, MBE. ISBN 630. £5.95.

TROOPSHIP TO CALAIS by Derek Spiers. ISBN 3395. £11.95.

TWO HALVES OF A LIFE by Doctor Kary Pole. ISBN 509. £5.95.

US BARGEMEN by A.S. Bennett. ISBN 207. £6.95.

A VIEW OF CHRIST'S COLLEGE, BLACKHEATH by A.E.O. Crombie, B.A. ISBN 223. £6.95.

LARGE FORMAT PICTORIAL PAPERBACKS

ARE YOU BEING SERVED, MADAM? by Molly Proctor. ISBN 3174. £3.50.

BEFORE AND AFTER THE HURRICANE IN AND AROUND CANTERBURY by Paul Crampton. ISBN 3387. £3.50. BARGAIN £1.95.

THE BLITZ OF CANTERBURY by Paul Crampton. ISBN 3441. £3.50.

CANTERBURY BEFORE THE BLITZ by Paul Crampton. ISBN 3662. £4.95.

CANTERBURY THEN AND NOW by Paul Crampton. ISBN 359X. £3.95.

CLIFFE IN OLD PHOTOGRAPHS by Allan Cherry. ISBN 362X. £3.95.

EAST KENT FROM THE AIR by John Guy. ISBN 3158. £3.50.
EAST SUSSEX RAILWAYS IN OLD POSTCARDS by Kevin Robertson. ISBN 3220.
£3.50.
GEORGE BARGEBRICK Esq. by Richard-Hugh Perks. ISBN 479. £4.50.
HEADCORN: A Pictorial History by the Headcorn Local History Society. ISBN
3271. £3.50.
KENT TOWN CRAFTS by Richard Filmer. ISBN 584. £2.95.
LENHAM AND BOUGHTON MALHERBE IN OLD PHOTOGRAPHS by Jean
Cockett and Amy Myers. ISBN 3646. £3.95.
THE LIFE AND ART OF ONE MAN by Dudley Pout. ISBN 525. £2.95.
THE MEDWAY TOWNS FROM THE AIR by Piers Morgan and Diane Nicholls. ISBN
3557. £4.95.
MORE PICTURES OF RAINHAM by Barbara Mackay Miller. ISBN 3298. £3.50.
THE MOTOR BUS SERVICES OF KENT AND EAST SUSSEX — A brief history by Eric
Baldock. ISBN 959. £4.95.
OLD BROADSTAIRS by Michael David Mirams. ISBN 3115. £3.50.
OLD CHATHAM: A THIRD PICTURE BOOK by Philip MacDougall. ISBN 3190.
£3.50. BARGAIN £1.95.
OLD FAVERSHAM by Arthur Percival. ISBN 3425. £3.50.
OLD GILLINGHAM by Philip MacDougall. ISBN 3328. £3.50.
OLD MAIDSTONE Vol.3 by Irene Hales. ISBN 3336. £3.50. BARGAIN £1.95.
OLD MARGATE by Michael David Mirams. ISBN 851. £3.50.
OLD PUBS OF TUNBRIDGE WELLS & DISTRICT by Keith Hetherington and Alun
Griffiths. ISBN 300X. £3.50.
OLD RAMSGATE by Michael David Mirams. ISBN 797. £3.50.
PEMBURY IN THE PAST by Mary Standen. ISBN 916. £2.95.
A PICTORIAL HISTORY OF COOLING AND CLIFFE by Allan Cherry. ISBN 376X.
£3.95.
A PICTORIAL STUDY OF ALKHAM PARISH by Susan Lees and Roy Humphreys.
ISBN 3034. £2.95.
A PICTORIAL STUDY OF HAWKINGE PARISH by Roy Humphreys. ISBN 328X.
£3.50.
A PICTUREBOOK OF OLD NORTHIAM by Lis Rigby. ISBN 3492. £3.95.
A PICTUREBOOK OF OLD RAINHAM by Barbara Mackay Miller. ISBN 606. £3.50.
REMINISCENCES OF OLD CRANBROOK by Joe Woodcock. ISBN 331X. £3.50.
ROCHESTER FROM OLD PHOTOGRAPHS — see under hardbacks.
SMARDEN: A Pictorial History by Jenni Rodger. ISBN 592. £3.50.
STEAM SCENE AT TONBRIDGE by Mike Feaver. ISBN 3670. £3.95.
THOMAS SIDNEY COOPER OF CANTERBURY by Brian Stewart. ISBN 762. £2.95.
TRANSPORT IN KENT 1900-1938 by Eric Baldock. ISBN 3603. £3.95.
WEST KENT FROM THE AIR by John Guy. ISBN 3166. £3.50.

STANDARD SIZE PAPERBACKS

BIRDS OF KENT: A Review of their Status and Distribution by the Kent Ornitho-
logical Society. ISBN 800. £6.95.
BIRDWATCHING IN KENT by Don Taylor. ISBN 932. £4.50.
THE CANTERBURY MONSTERS by John H. Vaux. ISBN 3468. £2.50.
THE CHATHAM DOCKYARD STORY by Philip MacDougall. ISBN 3301. £6.95.
CHIDDINGSTONE — AN HISTORICAL EXPLORATION by Jill Newton. ISBN 940.
£1.95.
A CHRONOLOGY OF ROCHESTER by Brenda Purle. ISBN 851. £1.50.
THE CHURCH AND VILLAGE OF TUNSTALL by Arthur A. Midwinter. ISBN 3697.
£3.95.
COBHAM. Published for Cobham Parish Council. ISBN 3123. £1.00.
CRIME AND CRIMINALS IN VICTORIAN KENT by Adrian Gray. ISBN 967. £3.95.

CYCLE TOURS OF KENT by John Guy. No. 1: Medway, Gravesend, Sittingbourne and Sheppey. ISBN 517. £1.50.
EXPLORING KENT CHURCHES by John E. Vigar. ISBN 3018. £3.95.
EXPLORING SUSSEX CHURCHES by John E. Vigar. ISBN 3093. £3.95.
FLIGHT IN KENT. ISBN 3085. £1.95.
FROM MOTHS TO MERLINS: The History of West Malling Airfield by Robin J. Brooks. ISBN 3239. £4.95.
THE GHOSTS OF KENT by Peter Underwood. ISBN 86X. £3.95.
HAWKINGE 1912-1961 by Roy Humphreys. ISBN 3522. £8.95.
A HISTORY OF CHATHAM GRAMMAR SCHOOL FOR GIRLS, 1907-1982 by Audrey Perkyns. ISBN 576. £1.95.
THE HOP BIN by Geoff & Fran Doel. ISBN 3735. £5.95.
IN BAGGY BROWN BREECHES by Norah Turner. ISBN 3654. £4.95.
KENT AIRFIELDS IN THE BATTLE OF BRITAIN by the Kent Aviation Historical Research Society. ISBN 3247. £5.95.
KENT AND EAST SUSSEX UNDERGROUND by The Kent Underground Research Group. ISBN 3581. £5.95.
KENT COUNTRY CHURCHES by James Antony Syms. ISBN 3131. £4.50.
KENT COUNTRY CHURCHES CONTINUED by James Antony Syms. ISBN 314X. £5.95.
KENT COUNTRY CHURCHES CONCLUDED by James Antony Syms. ISBN 345X. £5.95.
KENT INNS AND SIGNS by Michael David Mirams. ISBN 3182. BARGAIN £2.50.
LET'S EXPLORE THE RIVER DARENT by Frederick Wood. ISBN 770. £1.95.
LETTER TO MARSHY by Barbara Trigg. ISBN 3727. £3.95.
LULLINGSTONE PARK: THE EVOLUTION OF A MEDIAEVAL DEER PARK by Susan Pittman. ISBN 703. £3.95.
MARDEN: A WEALDEN VILLAGE by Phyllis Highwood and Peggy Skelton. ISBN 3107. £4.95.
MUMMING, HOWLING AND HOODENING by Geoff & Fran Doel. ISBN 3743. £3.50.
OFF THE BEATEN TRACK by Geoffrey Hufton. ISBN 3751. £3.50.
ONE DOG AND HER MAN by Ted Wright. ISBN 3719. £5.95.
PENINSULA ROUND (The Hoo Peninsula) by Des Worsdale. ISBN 568. £1.50.
PRELUDE TO WAR: Aviation in Kent 1938-39 by KAHRS. ISBN 3476. £2.50.
RADIO KENT GARDENERS' GUIDE by Harry Smith and Bob Collard. ISBN 3549. £3.95.
SAINT ANDREW'S CHURCH, DEAL by Gregory Holyoake. ISBN 835. 95p.
THE SCHOOL ON THE BALL FIELDS (CRANBROOK) by Mary Standen. ISBN 3638. £5.95.
SHORNE: The History of a Kentish Village by A.F. Allen. ISBN 3204. £4.95.
SIR GARRARD TYRWHITT-DRAKE AND THE COBTREE ESTATE, MAIDSTONE by Elizabeth Melling B.A. ISBN 3344. £1.50.
SITTINGBOURNE & KEMSLEY LIGHT RAILWAY STOCKBOOK AND GUIDE. ISBN 843. 95p.
STEAM IN MY FAMILY by John Newton. ISBN 3417. £4.95.
STOUR VALLEY WALKS from Canterbury to Sandwich by Christopher Donaldson. ISBN 991. £1.95.
TALES OF VICTORIAN HEADCORN — see under hardbacks.
TARGET FOLKESTONE by Roy Humphreys. ISBN 3514. £7.95.
WADHURST: Town of the High Weald by Alan Savidge and Oliver Mason. ISBN 3352. £5.95.
WARTIME KENT 1939-40 compiled by Oonagh Hyndman from the BBC Radio Kent broadcasts. ISBN 3611. £6.95.
WHERE NO FLOWERS GROW by George Glazebrook. ISBN 3379. £2.50.
WHO'S BURIED WHERE IN KENT by Alan Major. ISBN 3484. £5.95.